MW00571773

LITTLE WONDERS

THE WONDER OF

FRIENDS

Phyllis Hobe

The C.R. Gibson Company
Norwalk, Connecticut 06856

LITTLE WONDERS

The Wonder of Mom
The Wonder of Dad
The Wonder of Friends
The Wonder of Babies
The Wonder of Little Girls
The Wonder of Little Boys

Published by The C.R. Gibson Company,
Norwalk, Connecticut 06856

Printed in the U.S.A.
Designed by Deborah Michel

ISBN 0-8378-7704-0
GB404

A friend makes
you feel as if the
whole world
loves you.

Friends don't think it's funny to make fun of you.

A friend lets you ride
his new bike around
the block.

Friends can make
snowballs faster
than you can
throw them.

When a friend is pitching,
your batting average goes up.

❈━⟨⟩━❈

Friends can't stay mad at you.

$\mathcal{J}$ust because a
friend doesn't make
the team, doesn't mean
he'll stop cheering
when you do.

A friend keeps
you company
when your parents
ground you.

You can
count on a friend
to understand you—
even when you don't.

A friend always knows
what you need to hear,
and when you need
to hear nothing.

A friend remembers
doing something
more foolish
than what you just did.

A friend will
sleep on the sofa
and give you
the bed.

Friends don't intrude
on your life,
but they do keep
an eye on it.

Friends don't
measure your caring by
the amount of time that
you spend together.

☞ A friend who's always on time can have a friend who's always late,

━━━━━

☞ a friend who's methodical can have a friend who never makes plans,

☞ a friend who's serious-
minded can have a friend
who's lighthearted...

＋━┥┝━＋

☞ friends don't have to be
alike—they know how
to enjoy their differences.

You can tell a
friend how you
feel without saying
a word.

A friend is a
welcome mat,
but never a
doormat.

A friend understands
when you hurt too
much to talk...
and knows that just
being there
makes it hurt less.

When friends wear the same size clothes, they double their wardrobes.

FRIENDS DON'T TELL
YOU TO CHEER UP
WHEN YOU'RE
FEELING DOWN...

THEY DON'T OFFER
SOLUTIONS TO PROBLEMS

YOU DON'T WANT
TO SOLVE...

THEY DON'T INTERRUPT
WHEN YOU WANT
TO TALK...

THEY DON'T TRY TO
REASON WITH YOU
WHEN YOU'RE BEING
UNREASONABLE...

THEY'LL CHUCKLE ALONG

WHEN YOU CAN'T STOP
LAUGHING...

AND THEY'LL TELL
YOU WHEN TO
STOP THE NONSENSE.

Shopping together
is a real test
of friendship.

A friend is happy
when you are.

When you're broke,
a friend can treat
you to lunch
without making
you feel you owe
him something.

A friend can give
you a present
without expecting
one in return.

Your friends probably won't like each other as much as they like you.

*F*riends aren't blind
to your faults—
but they can see
beyond them.

A LETTER
FROM A FRIEND
CAN MAKE
YOUR DAY.

A friend will laugh
at your jokes
no matter how
many times you
repeat them.

A friend remembers
the way you were,
but won't insist
you stay that way.

A friend never asks, "What did you do to your hair?"

A friend won't
hang up on your
answering machine,
or when you put
him on hold.

A friend won't
tell you how to drive,
no matter how white
her knuckles get.

Friends love to give
you surprise parties—
even when you know
what they're up to.

A FRIEND IS THE ONLY PERSON WHO CAN MAKE YOU LAUGH AFTER A BROKEN ROMANCE.

Eating out with a friend takes at least three hours.

Friends can be
more patient with
your kids than
you can.

Friends know
there is no such
thing as constructive
criticism.

Friends aren't
interested in your
excuses—
they're interested
in you.

There is no bigger grin than that of a friend with good news.

When you ask a friend where he wants to go for dinner... he'll usually choose your favorite restaurant.

A friend knows
where your panic
button is,
but never pushes it.

A friend is more likely to give back the money she borrowed than the book you loaned her.

Friends can tell the truth
without hurting you.

Friends take very good care of
your hopes and dreams.

A friend remembers
your pet peeves...
your favorite colors...
the songs you like...
and ignores the
times you forgot to
remember hers.

A vacation with
a friend is not only
more fun, but also
less money.

*Friends can
turn arguments
into laughter.*

When you have
doubts about yourself,
call your friends,
because they'll have
confidence in you.

Nothing hurts as much as hurting your friend... nothing heals as much as being forgiven by your friend.

When a friend
moves away,
part of your history
goes with them.

Seeing an old
friend makes you
feel whole.